# There Is a Future

## *A Year of Daily Midrash*

poems by
# Amy Bornman

PARACLETE PRESS
BREWSTER, MASSACHUSETTS

2021 First Printing

*There Is a Future: A Year of Daily Midrash*

Copyright © 2021 by Amy Bornman

ISBN 978-1-64060-613-5

The Paraclete Press name and logo (dove on cross) are trademarks of Paraclete Press, Inc.

Library of Congress Cataloging-in-Publication Data
Names: Bornman, Amy, 1993- author.
Title: There is a future : a year of daily midrash / poems by Amy Bornman.
Description: Brewster, Massachusetts : Paraclete Press, 2021. | Summary:
  "Debut poetry collection from a new poet still in her twenties, each
  poem from the perspective of a midrash on life and Christian
  scripture"-- Provided by publisher.
Identifiers: LCCN 2020036340 (print) | LCCN 2020036341 (ebook) | ISBN
  9781640606135 | ISBN 9781640606142 (epub) | ISBN 9781640606159 (pdf)
Subjects: LCGFT: Poetry.
Classification: LCC PS3602.O7656 T47 2021  (print) | LCC PS3602.O7656
  (ebook) | DDC 811/.6--dc23
LC record available at https://lccn.loc.gov/2020036340
LC ebook record available at https://lccn.loc.gov/2020036341

10 9 8 7 6 5 4 3 2 1

Published by Paraclete Press
Brewster, Massachusetts
www.paracletepress.com

Printed in the United States of America

*to Isaiah.*

*you are bright city.*

*Turn it and turn it, for everything is in it.*
*Look deeply into it, and grow old with it,*
*and spend time over it, and do not stir from it,*
*because there is no greater portion.*

**—Rabbi Ben Bag-Bag**

# contents

Me    Debbie    9/14    Matthew 24 + 25    21st    28th    13th

# introduction

In the middle of 2018, I started reading the Bible every day. After a lifetime of Christian schooling and church-going and small groups and Bible class and homework, I felt like I'd read the Bible backward and forward. But I hadn't. I'd studied it in pieces, but I hadn't read all of it. After all that time thinking about it, *reading* the Bible felt like an interesting project to take on. So I began with the Daily Office in the *Book of Common Prayer*, reading what was appointed for the day each morning.

At the same time, I started reading poetry daily too, for the first time in my life. Denise Levertov, Jane Kenyon, Mary Oliver, Wendell Berry, Marie Howe, Kathleen Norris. The combination of these two sets of daily readings, the poets and the Scriptures, felt like, in chemistry, when you combine two elements and suddenly there's a dramatic fizzing spilling all over the table. Something started bubbling in me. My logical conclusion: I needed to practice writing poems, and I needed to keep reading the Bible. I needed to stir the pot as things were simmering wildly, for fear that if I didn't there'd be a big mess, a boiling over.

I remembered a friend in college telling me about the Jewish practice of midrash: an interpretive act of seeking answers to questions that are unanswerable, a way for rabbis and other God-wrestlers to interpret the text, trying to reconcile inconsistencies and contradictions, helping to bridge the gap between it and the people trying to understand it. Midrash is a practice in study and imagination. It began as a rabbinical tradition, but modern Jewish midrash is extended to the people and often expressed through art, poetry, prose, music, and theater. Midrash, at its heart, is the people of God honoring the text by *wondering about it*, aiding their minds by imagining what could fill the holes.

All of this captivated me—the spaciousness, the daring risk. Coming from my faith background in Evangelical Protestantism, where Scripture is taught to be inerrant and every bit of text is *true* somehow, where every question has a systematic-theology answer found in some commentary somewhere, I was astounded that midrash was not so concerned with that kind of truth and is, in nature, imaginative. Midrash plumbs the depths of *poetic truth*, a different creature entirely, but still truth. I began writing midrash poems, tenderly, with breath, hoping that I could borrow the term and inspiration without ruffling too many feathers—I'm not Jewish, after all. I hadn't written many poems before, just a lot of prose, mostly essays, so I began trying on poetry like a new shoe, walking in it around the room.

This was December. Each day I would read the passages assigned to the day in the daily office then write some sort of poem about something I read. Sometimes the poems linked several of the appointed passages, and sometimes they focused in on one story, or even one line. I made few rules for myself, except that I keep doing it, keep showing up. And I did, nearly every day, for a year. I took a big break in November, feeling the mental fatigue of having written so many poems and reading so much of the Bible, feeling the dread of all that was happening in the world. That month, I wrote poems at church instead, scribbling in my pew. Some days, the poems were truly terrible. Some days, I'd write three or four versions until I worked out what I was really trying to get at. Some days, the poems rang like a bell, clear and bright, as if someone else had written them. Those were the best days.

The poems in this collection are chronological, following my year of daily midrash poem-writing, from December to December, one Advent to another. When I read them in order, I see a mind sincerely changing, a new person being born, a deconstructed and renewed faith, the poetry keeping me in although the Bible kept confounding and confusing me out. The project meant I couldn't escape the terrible things in the Bible: murders, plagues, wars, rapes, genocide. I began to *understand* God less and less but *wonder about* God more and more, imagining an extraordinary and spacious gray. As an experiment, I willfully forgot, set aside, all the dogma I'd learned as a child, considering bald belief and poetic truth instead. The Bible was ripe with poetry, and I was ripening with it.

For so long, as a girl growing into a woman coming of age in my faith, I had practiced so much restraint, spent so much time listening and assuming that the person speaking was right. As a poet, I felt differently. I didn't want to be silent anymore. I couldn't be. I had to put myself in the poems and admit that I didn't know how to make sense of things. Into the poems burst my fear, my anger, my feminism and mysticism, my dissatisfaction with the church as it is, my grief over climate change, for refugees, for a harmful government, my hope for justice for the poor and marginalized, my questions about self and art, my frustration with money and capitalism, my dying faith kept alive by the fruit of Jesus, and my *experience*, suddenly now important where before it had always felt irrelevant. What amazed me was that all of these things echoed back to me from the text, a conversation of ancient and modern hope and sorrow.

I found myself thinking a lot about the apocalypse, the end of the world. It's hard not to do this when you actually read the Bible, as it's so woven throughout it. Those are the parts I'm naturally drawn to most, since they're already poetry. But, even more, I thought about the future. This was a surprise. The world is so crazy right now that it feels daring to even imagine a future anymore. Maybe it has always felt that way—I won't assume that now is any different or more terrible than any other time. But the Bible demands it, this imagination of the future. The Bible carries the future like a jewel, a pearl, a mustard seed, or maybe like a cursed fig, one that refuses to grow. Each time the Psalms would cycle back through to Psalm 37, every two months, and I'd read again, "there is a future for the man of peace," I felt my hope restored.

My belief wavers. I'm considering the facts over and over and nothing makes any sense. I'm more sure of that than ever before. Still, there is a future. It seems to me that Jesus and the future are one and the same. And I still believe in the future. In fact, it may be the thing I believe in most.

Temple was destroyed 70 Ab

TAke heed that No one deceives you
see that you are Not troubled
  for all these things must come to
  Pass
Beginning of Sorrows
  false prophets
   Lawlessness, Love of many will grow cold
Gospel will be preached as a witness to
   all Nations, and then the end will come
abomination of desolation takes place on
the jewish temple


people in Judeah should flee

for those who thought everything was
  fullfilled. Could not have been because
   the temple was destroyed in 70 AD

# from the fig tree
*matthew 24*

when it all melts, everything,
and the coffee won't stay in the cups,
that's when you'll know.

when you lose the sun, can't
find it, and the moon is also
lost and it's all a star instead,
that is when.

when your clothes all turn to sackcloth
and the ashes won't rub off and you go to
work but there's no one there
and at every tree a snake,
then.

when you walk to the garden and
meet angel with sword
who won't let you in even though
it's your home. when you're living in
tents near a border you'll cross,
near a wall that you're willing to climb.
when your mother is lost, so no one to
call, when your hair's fallen out and
the water is gone. when the cars are
abandoned and the dogs roam the streets,
you still laugh more than weep, can't figure out why.

*Disciples knew that Jesus was the messiah & the temple would be destroyed & the kingdom was coming. They did not understand other events would occur*

*Emphasis was on the necessity of faith + obedience even in times of sorrow + suffering*

*24:16-28 There would be a great tribulation before Jesus came only the father knows the day + hour. Christs coming will surprise everyone.*

*24: 32-35 When the branch has already become tender + puts forth its leaves you know that summer is near fig tree has a pattern*

1

when in the night there's a knock
at the door and the light seeping in
from the crack underneath.

that's when you'll know.

## you shall be a blessing
*zechariah 8, psalm 55, psalm 139, matthew 25, revelation 6*

meet me in my house at the bottom of the sea.
meet me in my mountain house, where we will
tremble and sing as the sky slides shut and
the moon turns red and the cars won't start
and the stars blink and drop.

meet me in my dove-house, fly away with me,
oh children whose names are
wait and start, i'll keep
the light on, put the fear out,
and lock my hate in a chest in the
attic to rest a while, and be.

come, please, to my treetop house
where i will make you herbal tea
and we can sit on the porch of my
gut and wait for eternity.

# philip's answer
*john 14, psalm 92, isaiah 55*

jesus said to him,
"have i been with you so long and you still do not know me,
   philip?"

your thoughts are
the great mystery
of my life. your thoughts
are the interior of myself,
the stuff i was made of,
the place through the mirror
where the image of me
shines forth, full of
you. i don't know you
and i wish with all
of my being that i could.
your thoughts are not my
thoughts, my thoughts are
thin and silty, with debris and
clouds and bits of destruction laced
throughout so your thoughts, pure and
milky, are such a beautiful dream I can
imagine if i try. it takes all of
my effort, my hopeless concentration,
and i can tell few people go there
to that quiet holy place
where your thoughts live

in them, too. to know that
the fullness of yourself
is within my own being is
almost troublesome to me
because of how little i
remember that and let
your thoughts spill out
of my mouth. your thoughts
are the great mystery
of my own, human, life.

i will give everything i
have to hear them spoken aloud.

# eve
*genesis 3*

thank you for
the wisdom i stole
and now hold like an
infant bird with hollow
bones i stand in the
beginning of fear here
is the world on the head of
a pin and i understand
and i weep alone
i only wanted to have
something to talk about
when we walked in the
garden together to stand
eye to eye with you rise
to your stature and
now the wanting is bigger
than it was more whole than
it was it's the joy
of my life to wait the pain of
my life to wait

# nathanael

*john 1, psalm 18*

i was completely
alone under the fig
tree, breathing deep
and with ease and
weeping for my life
and the world. under
the fig tree, it was
just me and some
gentleness i couldn't
name and the
mystery, breathing,
a hand on my back. it was
as if the air were thinner
and brighter in that
dim space under the
canopy, as if i could
sense that my life
could be good if i only
kept looking at, what?
and i watched the leaves
flutter in the wind and
i watched a bird land
and call and i closed
my eyes and opened
them again and could
have stayed there for
the rest of my life

but i knew i should
stand up and walk.

(and now i wonder)
was it your hand? what
greater thing than this,
you here, could i ever
live to see?

# the wedding at cana
## john 2

see mary at the wedding
watch her son across the
room with his friends,
watching the dancing,
servers whispering,
glancing down into their
pitchers of wine.

see mary look longer, see
jesus start breathing, start
standing slightly taller,
cheeks flushed, a tiny smile
beginning to grow. he laughs
at a joke, at a child who's
singing, he catches his
mother's eye, and he nods.

so mary walks over and they
share a small moment where
they both know a secret at
this wedding near their town.

and at once they're
back home in a memory where jesus,
just an infant, nursed at her breast,
she whispering his true name.
now, that same secret, and the

*What does Jesus mean when he said "My hour has not yet come"*

*Why did John chose to Record this miracle?*

*Mary knew Jesus could solve the problem*

*The hour to reveal himself He came with a purpose*

*John calls the miracles as signs they are recorded to show who Jesus is*

*Jesus was a people person He spent time with the common people*

*Jesus was humble and a Servant*

9

flutter in their chests, music
only the two of them could hear.

the water becomes wine and
the party keeps going, and the
dancers keep dancing and the
servers are amazed. and
mary can't stop laughing to
herself, a little giggle. all these
years she had been waiting for
this party to begin.

## flood poem

*genesis 7, psalm 114, ephesians 4*

blotted out like a mistaken word,
erased like a graphite smudge.
cancel this village, snuff out those
wolves, rabbits, lions, lambs,
and drown the trees too.
tremble, o earth, at the
presence of the lord, at the
presence of the one who destroys.
see the rock you are standing
on gush underneath you, see
families on housetops weep with
birds who can't land. full like a
cup to the tips of the mountains and
above. o water of life, will you
fill even this? o jesus, whose liquid
is love? tell me here as the mountain
is covered, is this the baptism you mean?

*[handwritten annotations:]*

Ephesians 4 grace has been given
put off falsehood & speak truthfully.

Ark

Tremble o earth at the presence of the Lord
Psalm 114 vs 7-8

How does this psalm encourage you at time of diversity

How does the imagery enrich your understanding of God's relationship with nature

Who closed the door? God Genesis 7:11-24

flood came when Noah was 600 yrs old
Rain fell for 40 days + nights
waters prevailed for 150 days

11

# I must decrease

*john 3*

i'll be a stem in the middle of a canyon.
i'll be a secret satellite orbiting the sun.
i'll be an ant on a leaf in the forest, a pill bug under a rock in the dark.
i'll be a grain of sand on the shore in the tide.
i'll be a pebble underwater in a stream.
i'll be the dust on the moon.
i'll be a leaf on a sycamore tree in the front yard of a house in a small
   rust belt town.
i'll be a tire on an appalachian hillside.
i'll be a screw in a door hinge.
i'll be a cactus on the side of a highway.
i'll be a wildflower in a meadow.
i'll be a crumbling wall, a gear in a machine.
i'll be a pigeon, a hawk flying alone.
i'll be a board game forgotten in a closet.
i'll be the bridesmaid who stands in the back.
i'll be a hair on a beloved child's head.
i'll be a coat that is no longer worn.
i'll be a coin that was dropped.
i'll be a kitten born in an alley.
i'll be a sock lost behind the dryer.
i'll be a pillow on the guest room bed, a bar of soap at the back of the cabinet.
i'll be a water jug carried for miles.
i'll be a thread in a favorite garment.
measure me smaller than the ruler has numbers. make me decimal,
fraction, sliver, speck, atom, none. if you'll only loom larger, i'll shrink in
your universe, be a small pulsing piece of the stuff full of you.

## the loaves and fish
*john 6*

in the morning, i'd looked at my lunch, disappointed.
i'd wanted some honey or milk or a cake.
i carried my loaves and my fish and my anger
for being so small and so tired of my life.
when i got to the mountain, i stayed in the back.
a man saw my lunch on the rock next to me
and brought me to jesus, who smiled, said, "how are you?
would you mind sharing your lunch with the crowd here today?"
i think i said nothing, i think i just stood there,
watched his hands moving over the loaves and the fish.
then his friends started walking and handing out lunches
and jesus came back and, would you believe it,
he winked?

# lot's wife
*genesis 19, psalm 58*

i looked back for the trees, that lane of tall oaks,
for the garden i planted, the tomatoes and pears,
yes, i looked back, for the kitten in the courtyard,
the stream and the stones, each blade of grass.
the brick buildings, the roads, that willow in the
square, the doorknobs and keys, the windows and doors.
the friends i have loved who are now surely dying.
if this city is wicked, then i'm wicked too, and i don't
know why i'm running away from my home. curse
my head for turning, curse my eyes for looking,
curse my mouth for opening to ask for grace,
but curse me more for escaping, for running this far.
let me please just look back and grieve as I go.
watch my heart vanish, watch it become dust,
watch my anguish be stillborn, watch me be swept away.
i'll stand here, just weeping, till my body is salty,
till i can't move my feet. let me die in the sun.

# simon peter says to jesus
*john 6*

lord, to whom shall we go?
i am a door and you are the key.
you are the bread and i am a
knife, i am a jar, you are water,
we are like brothers,
you're my beloved,
i never want
to leave your side,
my life begins with you.
lord, to whom shall we go?
there is no one else in the
world, not one. if you are
crazy then i'm crazy too.

## rehoboth
*genesis 26, john 8*

the worst day of my life and i am
the only woman in the place. eyes
of men squinting at me, looking in
corners for rocks to throw, already
imagining the arc of their arm.

once in my life i witnessed this ritual
and that once was enough for
a lifetime of dreams where the rocks
hit my body but i don't ever die, i just
keep being hit, never ending, alone.

i have a body. i am alive. what part
of me has run out of time? they've
decided i must no longer take up any
room, and maybe they're right. i've
been so often wrong.

a man i don't know in the dirt beside me,
please don't make this take longer, please
just let it be quick. he's moving so slowly
and it's agony waiting, till i notice
he's writing my name in the dust.

they listen to him and they walk away
slowly. my ears are ringing, i can't hear
what he said. my eyes are blurred looking
at the beautiful letters, all my most secret
nicknames spelled out by his hand.

16

# rachel's love song for jacob, the moment she sees him

*genesis 29, psalm 87*

you are bright city. you are
tall buildings, beautiful roads,
alleyways and lighted paths,
i am wilderness, faithfulness,
my life is to walk back and forth with
my sheep and now you'll walk with me,
move the stone away, ease my burdens,
fill my days, stay beside me, kiss my
face. this day is a hinge
in a door that's now wide,
please let it be simple, please let it be
calm like the sun at the dawn,
like a lengthening ocean,
all my springs are in you.

*[handwritten notes:]*

Genesis 29
Who did Jacob meet?

psalm 87

Genesis 26
Lord told Isaac not to go to Egypt
God promised to be with him
Land, more descendants, a blessing
why did Isaac Lie about Rebekah?
why did Isaac leave and go to Gerar?
what was the blessing Genesis 24-26
How does Isaac's story inspire us to
trust God during challenging times.

Dec 14th
karens

17

# mary anoints jesus' feet at bethany
*john 12, psalm 131*

silently, tenderly, she walks and
the room quiets with her footsteps.
she kneels at his feet and opens the jar
and the aroma fills the room. what last
murmurings there were subside and all faces
turn to look. martha comes out of her
kitchen, judas fumes, fidgety hands,
and jesus breathes and blinks.
he does not shift in his chair.
here, a hinge between heaven and
earth, and everyone can feel the
tear in the veil.

mary is focused though her hands shake.
with movements slow and deliberate,
she anoints his feet with oil,
the fragrance lifting up to the
ceiling, pooling in the corners,
filling every lung. here, a thick
audience, rapt to her work. here
a ritual so ancient she didn't have
to dream it up. she knows what
she's doing, she knows what it means,
she weeps as she goes, for in wisdom
she glimpses something too great and
too marvelous, too high to see.

mary pulls the ribbon from her hair
and everyone watches as it falls
down her back. she wipes the oil
off of his feet with her curls,
wild and loose, sensual, calm.
there is no sex here, only some sort
of love that hovers, floats higher than
their two human bodies, for one is
god and one is woman, and somehow
she has become powerful. the oil is a seal,
her hair is the earth, and now jesus
is sent, blessed, toward where he will die.

What was the dinner for in Bethany?
to celebrate the Lazarus. rising
from the dead
Who was the dinner for? the men
of the village women served
Since the oil was extreme — Mary
was very humble
wiping with the hair was rare
Lady Never Let down her hair in
public
Mary's heart went to the Lord &
She was expressing her feelings
Why did Judas object - He was shamed
by her simple and powerful display
of love
This is the only place in the New testament
Where Judas is mentioned as doing
Something evil
John #2:1-8
Why did they want to kill Lazarus - priests
thought many were going to Jesus because
of him
14 - Sat on a donkey; king is coming
the disciples did not understand
but later Remembered
Hosanna meant save Now    25:26                37-41
                              30      31-33      **19** 44-60

# vessels of wood and clay
*2 timothy 2*

i think of myself as a cup on a shelf,
a cream stoneware mug with the
flowers etched on, a thin layer of
dust like a blanket in my center.

please pick me up and wash me out!
please fill me with warmth,
with something that is a delight,
something that is a routine!
please, o please, hold me
in your hands!

Spirit of fear from God
does not come
+ we should not be ashemed
of our testimony to
Jesus

## closing on a house on ash wednesday

how would i feel if it burned down today, if
it all turned to ash, skin covered in soot?
remember you are dust, this house made of
wood that's now linked to your name, your
hope, not your faith. lie awake at night and
wonder if it's burning, if some spark lit it up
on this first day it's yours. store your treasures
in heaven, but you're chained still to earth,
and your dreams are of basement leaks like
terrible fountains. you wonder if you were
foolish to choose anything here, this house
is a hope in a slant-wise way onward, made
of nothing at all but the same dust as you.
fasting and thirst in a house with lead pipes,
earth sagging beneath, the whole city could
slip. i heard of a landslide just a few streets
northward, with a whole house sliding
down into the park. i'm attuned to catastrophe
like a bird on my shoulder, i hold a key in my
palm and pack up my things. the priest
marks my forehead with blessed ash, and i
imagine it's the rubble of this house that's
my hope. if it crumbles i will weep and go
on weeping, but how is that different than
the weeping i've done? see my hand sign
the papers, like i've signed in my blood.

i make death's house my home,
try to live in it still. see me
arrange the furniture, see me
open the blinds.

# river

*psalm 45, psalm 48, 1 corinthians 1*

i address my verses to some far-away thought,
a city whose measurements i could spend my life learning.
my tongue is like the pen of a ready scribe,
and i write down words i didn't know i knew.
i never wrote poems until one day i did, and it was
like i discovered a new river in me. walk about zion,
go number her towers, cross through her citadels,
wander her streets. count your paces, make it your business to say,
to write down, what you saw as you walked.
i saw a bird, a woman with a baby.
i saw a flood, some men selling their brother.
i saw a man who could cast out demons.
a child in a basket, a bush that was burning,
i saw a mountain, a beautiful garden,
i saw a river coming out of me.

# new lump

*1 corinthians 5*

become a new lump, it says,
which makes me laugh with a
puppy asleep beside me on the
couch. be unleavened, it says,
which surprises me because
don't we want to rise and puff
in the sun on the counter with some
glorious culture, some wonderful
yeast? be truthful and flat, it says.
won't this be the challenge
of my life?

## an opening
*genesis 43*

the bible is so often withholding,
its text keeping in a tight fist the
details i crave, the look on a face,
the witty remark, the private moment,
the smells and colors and lilting tune.
then you see joseph standing
once more in the same room
as benjamin, the only other son
of his mother, and the text tells us
he has to go to the other room to weep
and wash his face, to compose
himself before returning,

and suddenly i'm in front of every
bathroom mirror. suddenly, i know
this man whose face i've never
seen. suddenly, with a pop,
the book bursts open, and i
step through the door,
and i can see.

# mother god
*psalm 81*

open your mouth and i'll fill it.
come to the door and i'll open it.
put out your palm and i'll give you
a marble, cat's eye, streaked with
red and with blue. shiver your
shoulders and i'll wrap you
up. come to the piano and i'll
play you a song. tell me a joke
and i'll laugh. we'll go for a walk
on the path round the pond
when you come home restless,
late afternoon. we'll count the
geese as they fly. bring me some
flowers and they'll go in a vase.
a carton of eggs and i'll fry
them. for your empty cup,
i'll pour you some milk. for your
plastic spoon some cold
ice cream. ask for a story and
i'll find one to tell. come to the
door and i'll open it. open your
mouth and i'll fill it.

what i won't do is send you
off empty. what i won't do is
keep the door locked. when you're
far from home i sit and i wait.
expect to be filled with me.

# the syrophoenician woman
## mark 7

yes lord even the dogs under
the table eat the children's
crumbs, she says, and he looks at her
long, finally someone has surprised
him. he would have healed her
daughter either way because it is in his
nature to have mercy, but she squares
up to him, meets his eye, asks for
what she needs, and he goes on,
emboldened, to make all things new.

## garment psalm
*psalm 109*

take off cursing, peel it off
like some long sleeves gone
sticky with sweat, too tight
around the middle, collar
stretched and torn.
put on blessing instead,
the pale spun fibers, the
warmth of it, the coat
with pearl buttons. may
it soak into your bones,
the wellness and rightness,
the way you look in the
mirror, like yourself,
how you look when you're
all alone.

# the transfiguration
## mark 9

up on a mountain, at the top,
jesus stood and faced them and
his body became something new,
his skin shone and his clothes
became bright and white. a man like a
diamond, like a prism, like a wind chime,
he rang like a bell, the new wine suddenly
bursting the old wineskins, exploding
with warmth. said nothing, just
shone. the birds were silent, the
hawks and vultures landed to watch.
jesus whispering with elijah
and moses who touched his back,
like brothers after some time apart,
peter, james, and john stood
in their woven flax, wet with sweat,
hardly breathing, looking at their friend
and these others, all shining and real,
this man they had slept beside night
after night after night. they
memorized the way he looked, etched into
their minds how it felt to be there,
alone, with him like that, treasured it in their
hearts, told the story years later, while
breaking bread and sharing wine, the
best secret they ever had, the way
his glory looked.

*new wine skins stretched for the new wine*

*how it felt to be there*

*The silence*

*Jesus is bringing new things*

# burning bush
*exodus 3*

april's early days, the short weeks
when the forsythia blooms and everywhere
a burning bush. i first really noticed it
in college in the midwest, the illinois
sidewalks, bushes all pruned into
globes, learned its name, came to expect it.
forsythia for spring, the bush that only
burns in lent. when all is fasting, a feast.
for the rest of the year it's so ordinary,
in pittsburgh, especially, unruly, unkempt, the
sort of highway-side bush you wish weren't there.
but in april, each branch is articulated
with chartreuse. walking my dog
behind my house, the whole alley is lined
with bright blossoms like a wall of fire.
"here i am!" i say. i hide my face,
i take off my sandals, all the earth
is holy ground.

# parable of the tenants
*mark 12, lamentations 2*

the son takes his first step
again on the earth of his father's
vineyard, the sweet grape
smell of it, the rustle of the
leaves. he breathes it in,
counts the fruits, feels their
skin. stretches out his
measuring line to remember
the depth. he knows it will
all rot. he knows it will
kill him. the tenants have
forgotten the festival, have
neglected to bring the
fruit to the press. they've killed
every messenger, buried the bodies.
the son waits, breathing.
he sits on his father's dirt
right by the gate,
left hanging wide open.

# passover
*exodus 12*

kill your lambs, each family, at twilight
and collect the blood. take a bunch of hyssop
and dip it in the basin, touch the lintel and the two
doorposts with the blood, paint it onto the door frame
you walk through daily, the one you cut and nailed
yourself. have your children stand and watch you do this.
hand the hyssop to your wife, do it together.

go back into your house and have a feast, roasted
lamb, the sweetest smell, with bitter herbs and bread
without leaven. eat though you're anxious, though your
children sense the fear that twists around your neck.
eat with your belt on, your shoes tied, your wife wearing
her cloak indoors. all of you eat standing up, quickly, and
whatever you cannot finish, burn in the fire.

then, wait in the silent darkness, wait behind your door.
stay in your house, all together inside. you were told
that you'd be saved. there is something that could kill
you but it won't. you can't quite be sure it's true.
feel the softest breeze slipping under the door.
your family breathing together, not a soul asleep.
smell the burial spices on the edge of the wind.
hear the bells, the keys of death, as something
living passes by.

when, in the future, your children ask you what it meant,
when they wake with nightmares, hearing again the
distant weeping of the egyptian mothers, the way
your wife wept with them in your own house
in the dark though her children were alive against her body,
you won't know what to say, except,
*therefore let us keep the feast.*

and don't say alleluia.

## parting of the red sea
*exodus 14, psalm 3*

we do this all the time, you know,
walk straight through something
that washes someone else away,
feet on dry sand that really should
be underwater, floating atop on the
ark while others wait on rooftops
to drown. and there's no explanation,
no explanation, except that mercy is
extreme and keeps on choosing me
for no good reason i can determine
on my own. i cry aloud up the holy hill,
and i, tiny one, receive so many answers.

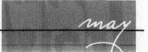

# when the women danced
*exodus 15*

i'm imagining this moment
when miriam the prophetess
grabs her tambourine and
begins to dance and all the
other women grab their
tambourines too and dance
with her. i'm remembering
all the times i've been in groups
of women dancing, the way we
know just what to do, the way
it's only for us, the way we face
each other, the way it feels
so nice to sweat because you're
dancing, to feel the flush on your
cheeks, to smile at one another,
to sing and to laugh, to shake a tambourine.
i don't think there's a more wonderful thing.

## *manna*
*exodus 16*

i forgot to write
a poem about the manna
this morning
and isn't that just typical
that the bread on the ground
you forgot to gather
spoils if you try
to keep it for even
one day?

i had an idea
that came with the dew,
now, in evening,
it's lost.

# moses talks with god
*exodus 20*

the people stood trembling at the base
of the mountain, watching the thunder
and the lightning and some wild blackness,
not quite dark, just out of sight.
moses, a stranger now, spent days climbing up and
down, ashen faced and thrilled, drinking water
after each trip, cup after cup, each time more
ravenous, more calm and crazed, both.
moses would climb back up again, and the
people would watch him, clutching each other's
hands. he climbed into the blackness
until he disappeared. they squinted up, they
craned their necks, they couldn't see moses
anymore.

# beatitudes
*matthew 5*

blessed are the peacemakers,
for it takes so very long.
blessed are the smallest,
for they shall be emboldened.
blessed are the generous,
for the blush pink on their cheek.
blessed are the song singers,
for there are always more songs.
blessed are women cooking meals,
for the tracks their feet make on kitchen rugs.
blessed are the merciful,
for they have new secrets,
ones i don't have.
blessed are the laughing ones,
see how full their pockets are?
blessed are the tigers,
for they are orange and black
and getting always softer,
more endangered than before.
blessed are the poor in spirit,
for there's a flame to be lit.
blessed are the pure in heart,
for, see? it's the top of the mountain.
blessed are the dancing girls,
the way their minds empty out,
the way they point their toes.

blessed is the grass and dirt,
for it's the greatest gift.
blessed are the driving men,
the logs they carry around.
blessed are those who mourn,
a cup of tea to pour in the morning,
blessed are those who hunger and thirst
for righteousness,
some satisfaction will come from somewhere,
i'm sure of it.
blessed is the color green,
i'm only just now seeing it.
blessed are the meek,
for they shall inherit the earth.

# an explanation
*psalm 50, exodus 34*

you thought that i was one like yourself.
you thought that i was stiff-necked like
you, prone to be unnoticing, unable to
choose. you thought that i was impossibly
soft, like one of my clouds. you thought
i was silent.

if i were hungry, i wouldn't tell you.
think of yourself, when you're hungry
you weep. if i were hungry, i wouldn't
tell you, for the world and all its
fullness is mine, the cattle on a
thousand hills, and i am always hungry.

before me is a devouring fire.
around me is a mighty tempest.
these, my intimates, my
council, my head, my garden.
don't you realize that
my storms aren't always visible?
don't you realize there's
so much you can't see?

you thought that i was one like yourself.
i am not. you and i are very different.
learn this carefully.

# moses' shining face
*exodus 34*

when moses came down
from mount sinai
with two tablets
in his hand,
he didn't know
that the skin of his face
shone because he'd
been talking with god.

the people were afraid,
and when they came
near and saw him face
to face, they asked him,
gently, if he could wear
a veil. they didn't know
what to say to someone
with a shining face.

moses looked for a mirror
and couldn't find one
anywhere. a basin of
water in the middle of
town, he removed his
veil and looked into it.
he couldn't see anything,
just the way the water
sparkles when the sun
sits on top of it, the way

the water keeps on moving,
carrying the sun.

# moving
*exodus 40*

you'll know it's time to leave
this place when the cloud is
taken up from over the
tabernacle, when it vanishes
into thin air. then you will take
down the screen for the door
of the tabernacle, then you will
pack up the golden altar in the
tent of meeting, put away the
fragrant incense in a saddlebag
or box. then you will pack up
the lampstand, put the table
on a cart. fold the veil, carefully,
though it will still surely wrinkle
on the way. leave the testimony
in the ark, but be sure to secure
the mercy seat. take off the
covering of the tent, un-spread
its canopy. take down the pillars,
the poles, the frames and bases.
pack it all up to be carried away.
look at the land where all of this
stood, say goodbye to this earth,
you'll never see it again. follow
the cloud to a new place. see
the grace in undoing everything
you've done.

## secret
*matthew 6*

but when you pray
go into your room and
shut the door and pray
to your father who is in
secret. but when you pray,
sit with your back against
the wall and tell no one
what you thought about there.
but when you pray, become
very still, or maybe dance,
hold the secret on the tip
of your finger, blow it into
the air. but when you pray,
look at a tree and keep on
looking, the leaves are always
moving, there's always some
kind of wind. but when you
pray, i don't care what you do,
i don't know at all what it's like
for you. i hardly know what it's
like for me to pray in secret
such secret things, the wordless
breathing i do in the mornings
when i'm almost still asleep.
i can't tell you about it at all,
i wouldn't know how to begin.

44

you know me, i love to tell.
everything i have i would give to you.
but there are some things i withhold
without even meaning to, some things
i can't find even within my own mind.
funny how easy it is to keep secret
the most incomprehensible things.

# gleaning
*leviticus 19, matthew 6*

look outside at the lush of green,
the vines love to grow, the fruit loves
to form and loves to be eaten.
when you reap the harvest of the land,
don't take the fruit on the edges,
don't gather the grain that
has fallen on the ground. don't strip
the vineyard bare, and don't pick
up the fallen grapes. leave them for the poor,
or the traveler, or the stranger.
leave the gate open and unlock the door.
unlearn your holding things back,
unpack all your storehouses,
leave it out on the curb.
don't you see we've gotten it terribly wrong
by pretending things are ours?

when you travel, when you're far from home,
when you look around and aren't sure
where you are, look for a light kept on,
a garden or a meadow. look for the ones
who have left something sweet for you to take.
if they've left nothing for you,
shake off the dust from your feet,
and keep going, with singing,
to find another place.

# flowers
*matthew 6*

consider the lilies of the field,
how they grow, they neither
toil nor spin yet they wear
such fine colors, they burst
out one morning as if from a
trap door. consider the peonies,
their careful handfuls, their
considered layers, their jewels
inside. consider the roses, they
smell so good. the hydrangea,
never without friends. the dandelion,
giddy even when unwanted, the
violet and bluebell and poppies
waving in the air. look at these,
who planted them? why should
you worry for even a moment
when such delicate things
go on surviving? why should you
worry for even a moment when
you know that the flowers will
come back next year? step out
in springtime and you'll learn
what I'm saying. impossible
to stand without wonder at
the foot of a flower.

# the door
*matthew 7*

i'm learning not to assume disaster,
i'm learning to hold out my hands,
asking for bread, and not expect
a stone. i'm learning to ask and
wait open for an answer instead
of dooming myself to silence,
thinking i'm always alone.
my greatest darkness is the fear i harbor,
my insistence that somehow the world
is not good. my greatest fear is that
the door will never open though i
knock and fling myself against it,
or wait across the hall
afraid to even go near.
i worry that the door is not a
door at all, that i'd swing it open
in a moment of boldness and
find a cement wall. ask, and it
will be given to you. seek, and you
will find. knock on the door with
the softest fist, put your ear to the
wood and listen for movement,
the soft swish of a garment, a
cup being lifted to lips, someone
cooking onions, a dinner being
prepared. something or anything
happening in the great mystery room.

if the door opened now you'd be flattened
by light. today, keep your hand on
the knob. imagine the threshold.
think about the moment when the door would
swing open, hinges creak.
how will it feel to see the knob so slowly turn?
you'll walk through and know, finally,
what it's like in that room.

# fruit
*matthew 7*

are grapes gathered from thorns,
or figs from thistles?
look at the table – a basket of
oranges, bright with oil, or
the wood gleaming bare?
      which is it?
you will know them by their
fruit, the sweet smell following,
an apple placed in the palm
of your hand, unmistakable in
its realness. in a bowl, there's
either some peaches or there isn't.
it's maybe more practical than i thought.
wherever jesus goes, bananas and
pears, like midas but sweet,
fruit everywhere he has touched,
a trail of berries like breadcrumbs
wherever his feet have been, fairytale
fruits appearing from nowhere,
juice like blood that drips and stains
      and satisfies.

# another explanation
*leviticus 26*

i see you live with panic,
with wasting and fever that
consumes the eyes and makes
the heart twist. i see you with
famine, being ruled by people
who hate you. i see you running,
always running, so afraid. i see
our heavens like iron and
our earth like bronze.

if you want to know what i want,
if you want to know what the
whole world is about, why things
are the way they are, i want
closeness with you. i want to
give you what I have. as close as
air is to skin, the unity of molecules,
their life together. if you walk in my
statutes in these dark strange
days, it's a way to be closer.
don't you see, if you'd come,
i'd give you everything i have.

## a canopy
*isaiah 4*

for over all the glory there will be a canopy,
a booth for shade by day, and a roof for
shelter by night. a glorious gauze over
your head, window-filled ceilings,
something beautiful up above. i noticed
last week a canopy at church, an
ornately carved wooden canopy
over the place where the gospel is
read. all of a sudden i wanted to stand
right under that wood, to make that
my home. as a child, i slept in a canopy
bed, pink fabric over me in layers every
night, no ceiling in sight, something warmer
instead, until i grew too old and took
the canopy off. this weekend, i stood
barefoot on a chair to decorate a wedding
arch with sheer white fabric, hydrangeas
and eucalyptus, stepping back to see if it
was even, making adjustments till
it all sat just so. for every blessing, a
roof over your head. a tree with many
leaves, a sky that is blue and thick,
an intact ozone, patched and whole.
wellness as a canopy right over our heads.
the opposite of nothing, something instead.
you look up and something wonderful is there.

## the owl and the sparrow
*psalm 102*

i am like a desert owl of the wilderness.
like an owl of the waste places;
i lie awake;
i am like a lonely sparrow on the housetop.

the psalms repeat every eight weeks
in the lectionary, cycle through over and
over and over. some i am bored of, some
i relish, some i write down every time in my book.

i am like a lonely sparrow on the housetop,
i am like a desert owl of the wilderness.
and am i? i must be.
it lifts from the page like a bird in flight,
like a small bird, alone, secret, singing a song,
like an owl in a wasteland, nothing living in
sight. am i those things? why
do i write it down every time,
a ritual of my pencil forming these words,
two months between?

these words are a poem for me.
i memorized them without meaning to.
they come to mind sometimes.
they must say something true.

# elegy for the earth

a found poem

*ecclesiastes 12*

before the sun and the light and the moon and the stars are
   darkened
and the clouds return after the rain,
in the day when the keepers of the house tremble,
and the strong men are bent,
and the grinders cease because they are few,
and those who look through the windows are dimmed,
and the doors on the street are shut –
when the sound of the grinding is low,
and one rises up at the sound of a bird,
and all the daughters of song are brought low –
they are afraid also of what is high, and terrors are in the way;
the almond tree blossoms,
the grasshopper drags itself along,
and desire fails, because man is going to his eternal home,
and the mourners go about the streets –

before the silver cord is snapped
or the golden bowl is broken,
or the wheel broken at the cistern,

and the dust returns to the earth as it was,
and the spirit returns to god who gave it.

# abundance
*matthew 17, psalm 78*

i wasn't made to be silent.
i will open my mouth in a parable,
i will utter dark sayings from of old,
talk about things i don't understand
with language that's incomplete.
i'll tell you what i heard somewhere,
i'll give you the coin i found
in the fish's mouth, the first one
i caught. he said it would be there
and it was. i went down to the water,
now it's in the palm of my hand.
i'll tell you everything i know.

# friendship
*numbers 12*

moses is no prophet. no, moses
is not merely a prophet, one i
speak to quietly, murmuring in
visions, in dreams, whisper secrets
in the wind, maybe misremembered,
misspoken, twisted, too proud.
no, moses is no prophet, moses is
my friend. with him i speak
mouth to mouth,
i stand at full height, he beholds
my form. to him i speak clearly,
not in riddles. moses has seen my
back. your jealousy deceives you.
do you wish to be my friend,
or merely to have what he has?
would you rather listen or speak?
moses is meek, moses comes back
to me again and again, ready to hear.
he has shown me himself, and i
behold his form. you don't know him
at all. do you wish to be a prophet
or a friend?

# spies
## numbers 13

go spy on the land
that will be our home.
peek through the sumac
branches, the allium puffs.
see the meadow and wonder
if it's from another world, one
much like this one but with more
milk and honey. maybe where each
season is everlasting? where it's all of
them at once? string a grape vine along
a branch to carry back with you, some figs
and some pomegranates to show what you've
seen. the people are big there, but they'll be your
brothers or maybe they'll disappear in a puff of smoke.
caleb says we will take the cities, that it won't be too hard.
investigate what is to be, imagine living there,
building a wooden house, laying down the
fruit on your own dining room table.
this is the first day of summer
all is still time-bound, and
we aren't there yet.

# says the quiet early vineyard worker
*matthew 20*

no, i don't wish i'd tarried in
the market till the last hour,
the best deal. the vineyard was
lovely all day, the sun through
the leaves on the vine. the
heavy fruit to gather, the songs
we sang as we worked. juice
on my hands and legs.

no, i don't wish i'd waited
longer, i'd only have wasted
my time with gossip and
worry and other things that
just stretch out the days, give
them circular shape. just as
much sweat, a different kind.
sleepiness that goes on and on.

no, i'm happy to work
if you'll have me, to have a
reason to stretch my arms
and legs. that's all that i need,
that's payment enough.
is there a better way to
spend a day? i'll be back
tomorrow, at your gates at dawn.

# the fig tree
*matthew 21, romans 6*

no fruit on the fig tree
and no place to hide when
jesus came walking, hungry
for fruit. his hands on the
limbs, he looked for a blossom
a small fig growing, one
nestled in the leaves.
but nothing, no fruit,
just the green splendid rustle.
no figs for a hungry man to
grasp in his hand,
a bride with no tenderness,
a bell with no ring,
a ball thrown far,
never landing anywhere.
do you know your proper use?
what have you done?
jesus cursed the fig tree
and it withered at once.

# parable of the wedding feast
matthew 22

you, by the river, on the back deck,
in the prison, will you come to the
party? the others would not come.

you, in detention camp, on the other side,
in the meadow grass, will you come
to the party with me?

you, on the golden street, the shopping
mall, the tall corn field, will you come to the
party? the others would not come.

you, at the top of the hill, other hemisphere,
baking loaves of bread, will you come
to the party with me?

you, drinking bright red wine, wearing
tennis shoes, holding babies close, in the
mountain air, in the arctic dark,
will you come to the party?
the others would not come.

you, in the air conditioning, the science lab, the grocery store,
you, in the yellow house, the tent and mat, the hotel bed,
you, grilling sausages across the street on your front porch,
you, with the thick black hair, the flower eyes, the wrinkle cheek,
you, with the little dog, the cardigan, the telephone,

you, beside me on the bus,
you, beside me in my bed,
you, somewhere I've never been,
will you come to the party with me?

# signs of the end of the age
*matthew 24*

and you will hear of wars and rumors of wars,
kingdom against kingdom, and there will be
famines and earthquakes in various places.
all these are the beginning of the birth pains.

how many wars? how many more rumors?
two earthquakes the other day near where
my friends live, and famines all over, the
food disappearing more quickly than the
hope. an ordinary day this month, 128 degrees
in parts of rural india. i heard that on the news.
the kids still play cricket. i heard that too.

this labor is long, it's deep and wide. we've
been laboring, and the pain will get worse.
were we born to bear it like this,
in long-suffering anguish, in fear for
the next wave of nausea and tightness?
was it meant to take this long,
to become so complicated, so risky,
like we could be rushed out of the birthing room,
emergency, at a moment's notice?
like it could all burst in a torrent of water
and blood spilled over the floor?
and you will hear of wars and rumors of wars,
you will see evil rulers and children murdered,
famines and earthquakes in various places,
you will see the ice melt and the storms come,

the heat drying up the greenest things.
you will miss the coral reef. you will dream
a cumulus cloud. keep waiting,
kept awake with your pains through the night.
we'll mother a new world someday.

# poem from matthew
## matthew 24

i can't write this poem
because i'm too sad to
write it. two men will
be in the field; one will
be taken, and one left.
two women will be
grinding at the mill;
one will be taken
and one left. where
will i be taken?
where is there to
go but here? what
does it mean to be
left? which one would
i want? sometimes the
mysteries thrill me, but
today i am sad about
more things than this.
i can't write this poem,
i can't start to string
word upon word without
feeling something swell
inside me, something
wordless and interesting,
something that gives me
nothing to do.

what does it mean
to be left?

# there is a future for the man of peace
## joshua 2, psalm 37

maybe rahab could see
the future in the faces
of the strangers, refugees,
fugitives, she hid
on her roof. maybe rahab
looked at them and saw
in their eyes and bodies,
hands and feet, some
renewal of the cosmos,
some vast beautiful way
to survive. maybe rahab
believed in the future,
maybe rahab clung to it
like a fable or myth, a
dream where there was
a scarlet cord tied around
the windowpane, a brush-
stroke of blood over the door
so death would pass over,
a woman surrendering her
body to give birth to
something holy so the
world could change,
expensive perfume in
an alabaster jar anointing the feet
of one who would be murdered,

it's all the same story and all
the same choice and maybe
she saw it all at once, like a flat
circle, like a pebble in her hand,
like a hazelnut, like a poem.
maybe rahab could see the future
and in the future she saw mercy.

# psalm 45
for brett foster

*psalm 45*

i tucked into your death like a stowaway,
stood in your last weeks with wide eyes
and open mouth. i never spoke to you, watched
you become more and more thin, watched your
friends whisper and wait. i was speaking your poems
out loud in a room full of people who loved you
the moment you died. was it then?
i couldn't reflect, i couldn't absorb, i was shocked
by the privilege to sit in your void, all of us
knowing exactly what had happened or would
happen when father martin left the room.
we kept speaking. was it then that
the mantle was passed and your poems
settled into me exactly like seeds in,
o bless me, good soil?
i can't read this psalm, this
*my tongue is like the pen of a ready scribe*
without seeing your soul like a flame,
flash then snuff, without hearing your
*tongue is the pen*, rushing to google to read it again,
to see your line breaks like a cairn placed by your hand.
i remember what you wrote.
i know your words better than most scripture,
most liturgy, memorizing them in your
last days because it's what we were doing.

i didn't mean for that to happen,
you happened to me, the strange fact that
i was enfolded into your life, or really only your
death, with some cosmic double-knots, so swiftly and
so sure. *there's a hypothetically bright future for everything,*
*each wounded creature that is bitten, or bites.*
it becomes more important with each
day that passes, the pressing need to sing
the same song as you, different voice.
hear, o daughter, and consider,
and incline your ear;
forget your people and your father's house.
your robes are fragrant with myrrh,
and aloes, and cassia, someone else's
burial spices. go on, daughter, and write.

# denial
*matthew 26*

the night has fallen and i say
three times, "i don't know!" and
i weep, bitterly, i feel it fall apart.
the rooster crows at me, with me,
for me, it crows my heart in two. i
betray three times a day.

the more i crack open the things
i sealed shut, the questions that
felt most dangerous, the places
where reason stops, the more i
say, "i do not know the man."
i have no answer for my soul,
i face myself and shrug.
it's always me, the questioner.
it's always my smartest self.

what of this faith that goes further?
like something outside of me,
like the inside of a poem, the
part you don't understand,
the detective in me who
could never resist a mystery.
i watch my feet keep walking
back up the mountain, back
toward the cross. i feel myself
always returning to the last place
on earth i want to go.

## pentecost

*acts 2, joel 2*

a flame on each of your heads
like incense, smoking little by little
with the sweetest scent of
sandalwood and jasmine and cedar.
in the last days the spirit will be
poured out onto the people,
children as prophets, your sons
and your daughters asking you
to change. young women seeing visions,
old women dreaming dreams. new
mysticism, see the tongues of fire
on their heads while they tell you
something new. signs and wonders,
moon like blood, sun like darkness,
smoke, flood, fire, melt, you'll hear
it come quicker each day, spreading
by word of mouth or hand to hand, not
crazy to wonder at the end of the
world anymore. and it shall
come to pass some sort of great healing
if you ask, as you burn, to be healed.
that's what they're talking about as the
lithe curls of sweet smoke rise daily
from their heads. they could burn up
but they don't, just smoulder.
healing as quickly as they
burn.

# teach me christ
*john 1*

if it isn't the opening of the
august roses, second bloom, to
teach me christ, then what will it be?
the sun sits on each leaf of the
maple tree out my window, the
tree that is sick with maple tar,
black spots on each leaf,
curling up, brown, early. the
sun sits on each leaf, the thin
green flesh becomes a window
for the light that is in the world,
the light that is felt and needed
and gathered but never understood.
the light that comes from far away
(we don't know where) and makes
it here to us. it falls on everything.

i know about love. i know
about poetry and standing
under a canopy of trees in
a creek, cold water running
over my feet, a child of
pennsylvania. i know all
the stories, but i'll read
them again to see if there's
something new this time.

# to whom shall we go?
*john 6*

simon peter answered him,
lord, to whom shall we go?
you have the words of eternal life,
you are the well, we are the bucket.
if there's someone else to go to,
tell us their name. to whom shall
we go to drink clean water, to
be filled with the heaviness of
all that is needed? i'll be the
arms that draw the water at
the well. i'll be the skin on
the arms. i'll be the throat that
drinks and drinks. i'll linger
near the stones even after
filling my bucket, lay my palm
flat against their cool
dampness just to feel
and feel and feel. tell me
where else would i go?
all of it is desert except you.

# job: cosmos
*job 9*

how can i begin to ask for help
when you are the one who has wounded me?

i have no good apart from you,
you have taken it all

to the place you have hidden the stars,
the frame where you stretched the heavens.

i am on another earth, the one
that is not loved by you.

to whom should I go?
may i speak? do you hear?

you are no man. there can be no conversation.
there is no logic, no hands, no eyes.

i don't know what to do with you.
you've made yourself make no sense.

i ask for help, you withhold the mercy, obtusely
grabbing the sun to keep it from rising.

you have shaken my earth out of place,
you have trampled the waves of my sea.

the laws of the physical world no longer apply
and i am alone, floating in space.

the black hole has opened,
this is my dense eternity.

## the nave

i take off my glasses at church
and see the nave as a painting
with thick globs of oil, golden
orbs where there are candles,
all softness, texture, shades of light.
i wish my ears could blur
too as if i were underwater,
to let me think and see more
dimly as the blueness holds
me up. in truth, my sight
is too clear and my hearing
is too good, too busy with
the details to see the enchantment
of the room. give me softness,
underwater. give me ocean, give me
lake. give me seaweed, give me
dolphin, give me coral, give me stream.
give me somewhere i can float.
do not make me see.

# jesus walking, it was winter
*john 10*

jesus walking, it was winter.
the feast of dedication was
in jerusalem. he was walking
in the colonnade of solomon,
perhaps remembering him,
some dim memory from another
part of himself. the people
surrounded him again, and
maybe he only wanted to be
alone, in the winter, in the
colonnade of solomon,
walking and feeling the
cooler air on his skin, thinking
about his skin and everything
he loved. he spoke to them,
he gave them his time, again
and again and again.
*everything you need to remember*
*will stick in you like a pin.*

# job: what name should I call you now?
*job 29-30*

o tornado god,

hurricane god,

bad weather god,
chaos god.

will you stop your
spinning and hear
my cry? you've tossed
me about too long.

o opposite god,

underside god,

deep down dark
and sadness god,

disaster god,
explosion god,
everybody weeping and shouting god.

what name should i call you now?

# job: do you know?
*job 38*

do you know when the mountain goats give birth?
do you observe the calving of the does?

no, you don't. only i am there.
the angels and me, we wait with
held breath, we surround the mothers,
the copper deer, laboring alone under
trees, in meadows. we sing the
song of newness as they crouch
and the infant deer are born.
there's a crack and a pause and
all of heaven sees and knows
and i bless the fawn as it stumbles
and stands for the first time in
its life, lifted by my gaze.

you don't know what it is like.
if you did, you'd be asking different questions.
job, there are secrets everywhere.

# job: the secret
*job 40*

i've shown you the whirlwind.
i've told you the secrets of the
world i love. the best parts of it,
i've given to you. i'm here.
we wrestle. you stayed past
the first bitter argument, you never
stopped asking your questions.
you didn't lie down and die.
you, behemoth,
you, leviathan.
there's no creature i'm more
proud of than you.

## exultate deo
*psalm 81*

by *the waters of meribah* do you mean my house
up the forty red stairs to the front porch where
i stand in the morning's 55 degrees feeling
at once big and small and so unsure of what to do?
by *testing* do you mean the dailiness, the way
we don't know when things will change? the
living that draws out over days and days and days?
you say, as i stand on my porch, bare feet,
*open your mouth wide, and I will fill it.*
so i stand, open mouth, my eyes on the fuschia
mums i bought in the suburbs to feel some
sort of passing of the seasons. i need them.
i stand on my porch and nothing happens at all.
my mouth is a cavernous place.

# the coming destruction
*micah 1*

i would speak like the prophets speak
and my speech would not be misplaced.
hear this, all of you. pay attention, o earth,
and all that is in it. the mountains will
melt. the valleys will split open like
wax before the fire, the way the candle
stands then spills, as easily as water
falls. the lord is coming to tread upon
the high places of the earth, and i don't
know what that means but there is
something happening and it would
be wrong to keep silent. for this i will
lament and wail. i will go stripped and
naked. i will speak too long in the wrong
places. i will be loud and shrill and
make lamentation like the jackals,
and mourning like the ostriches.
for the wound is incurable.
there is no health in us.
it has come here, to our neighborhood.
it has reached the gate of my people,
to america, pennsylvania, my very
own dear hills and my very own small
body within them begin to tremble with

loss. see the ancient stones weep
with me. i will not keep silent.

# this is no place to rest
*micah 2, luke 7*

arise and go for this is no place to rest.
there's poison in the water, lead leached from the pipes,
some terrible thing radiating from the very ground you walk on,
the houses are falling down, a blight that the vines crawl up
because they wish for all to be made whole again.
the earth did no wrong, it was you who made it foul and
dangerous, years and years of doing whatever you wanted
as if you were a god. so arise and go,
find another holy place (they all are) and treat it
like it's christ's own body because of course it is.
how gladly the earth dies for us because it
loves us, the molten light beneath our feet,
a silent humble heat without a name,
born in anonymity, too beautiful to look
away. be the silent minister, wash the
feet of the earth with your own
tears and hair as it dies and dies
and dies.

# the future
*micah 4*

if every sword were changed to plow,
if every spear to pruning hook, if the
energy and adrenaline of the world were
tuned to earth and leaf in specific places,
beloved and known as a child knows their
backyard where worlds are imagined,
if governments opened tight fists to reveal
the kernels of sorrow held within, if war were
no longer taught or mentioned, a curse word too
terrible to say. if every person sat under
their own vine, their own fig tree and
looked up at the sky and down at the
earth and no one made them afraid,
that is a future i dare to imagine with
the thin hope left in me, the gladness
that remains though it has every reason
to go. why do you cry aloud? has the
pain seized you now like a woman in
labor? here we writhe and groan together
in the strange euphoria of hard work,
o daughters of zion, we were made for
this child, the future we birth with blood
and shouts too slow to bear, the fear that
all may still be lost if we stop pushing
it onward, if we lay down and die.
arise and thresh, o daughter of zion.
climb the mountain, don't give up.

# the four winds
*micah 6, revelation 7*

o my people, my people, what have i done to you?
have i tired you out? are you weary, asleep?
will you answer me when i speak, do
you listen while you wait?

there are four angels who hold the four winds.
they stand in the cosmos's corners, white knuckled,
holding tight the power to harm the earth
and the sea and the trees and they keep their
eyes on me, they sing and sway and hold
the winds in their hands, their fists, and they
wait for me.

but what have i done to you, have i wearied you?
have you grown confused by how muddled it's
gotten? have you been waiting too long, have you
fallen asleep? i do not blame you. these are terrible times.
trace back in your memory to what i told you before,
the instructions i whisper when you look back at me.
do justice, love kindness, walk humbly at my side.
the things we teach to children, have you been doing them at all?

there are four angels who hold the four winds.
think of them while you wait, imagine the
strength of their hands.

## church poem

i sit in the pew, blue velvet cushion,
an interloper interested more in
sensation, blue velvet, than sermon.
if i were to tell you about the most
wonderful things, what would I say?
would i speak of a good land where
there is enough water and food, such
elemental bucolic wonders, would
that move you and me enough? i've
lost sight of what heaven could be
except for the loveliest idea, the
central core wonder that exists in
all natural things, things we
already possess. what would heaven be
but more of earth? even as the days
grow shorter and evening is spent
watching headlights float down the
hill across the valley,
falling asleep too early, earth is all
i've loved. could it be that we
already know all that we need to know?

i join in for the creed. i know it
by heart. the life of the world to
come, amen.

# horoscope

so funny now to think how
much it was drilled into me
as a child to reject the stars,
to never imagine they were
ordered or wise. so funny now
to reimagine them as something
real, to sit over pizza and cider
with friends and argue our signs,
try to make sense of the way
the sky was at the moment of
our birth. for if the stars were
arbitrary, if it meant nothing,
what is there to believe? i want
to believe it all. i want to imagine
that everything on earth knows
more than i do, turns and turns
and carries the timing of life.
instead of a doctrine of subtraction
give me a doctrine of everything
knows. give me the stars and
the heavens, looking down on me
with love and the fullness of time.
i've put a star in my window now
to remind everyone I'm alive.

## *future god*

god is a future, a safety
that exists against all odds
where we all stay alive
and can be together. god
is a city where we each have
a home that doesn't cost
too much. god is a family,
the dinner party without
argument, talking long
into the night around the
table, no one leaves.
god is no man, no woman,
no being, they're the hope
itself that we keep on having.
i have it, do you have it too?
god had a child and we
talked to him. god is water,
spilling. god doesn't wonder
what you're thinking about.
god needs no prayer to feel
important. god doesn't listen,
but rather speaks your words
with you. god is a future,
and i think god exists.

# god's thoughts on blood
*isaiah 1*

the red is shocking isn't it?
when you cut your skin and it
stains your linen garments, your
floors and wooden tables. i've
seen your blood on everything
and i can't take it anymore. i look
through my fingers at you, all
covered in the sticky red of
pain, your sacrifices. i see you
scrub and scrub on your hands
and knees, in the sink, at the river.
i'll send you snow in the middle of the
night. i'll send you cotton, i'll send
you milk. i'll send you lamb through
mother's blood, wash him off
in the stream until the red comes
off and you'll see he's whiter than wool.
he is different than you. you've done
all you could.

# how can you
*psalm 11*

how then can you say to me
fly away like a bird on a housetop?
if i could, i would. but where
would i fly to? no other home in
sight. everything is here, the earth is one.

## the vineyard
*luke 21, isaiah 5*

and there will be signs in the sun and moon
and stars and on the earth distress of nations
in perplexity because of the roaring of the sea
and the waves, people fainting with fear and
worry for what is coming on the world. i stand
in a vineyard with walls that have tumbled
down, one that has not been pruned or hoed,
the wild grapes all twisted and thorny like a
secret in this place. where's the one that built
it? what shall i make of this waste?

# the year that king uzziah died
*isaiah 6*

and all the while the seraphim stood
and i couldn't imagine what they were
thinking of me and my ashen lips, my
tremor at the coal, my thin voice shouting
"here i am, send me." i'm not sure they
believed me, their golden many
faces calm and wide, never betraying
their minds. and couldn't they be sent?
wouldn't they want to in all their strength
and beauty? i tried to explain to them,
to everything in the room (even the throne,
the namelessness on it) that i am unclean,
we are all unclean, and then somehow i was
the only one there who said anything at all,
somehow i was just a voice talking to anyone
who would hear.

# acknowledgments

Thanks always to *Workout* and Wheaton College's Arena Theater, the place I learned poetry without even realizing it, where my prayers are stored in the walls. Thanks especially to Mark Lewis for so many things, including the opportunity to participate in KJV, where my love of the text of the Bible was rekindled.

Thanks to Brett Foster, whose words have settled into my walls like prayers.

Thanks to the poets who came before me and changed my mind about poetry by writing poems that rang like bells and kept ringing in my mind.

Thanks to Church of the Resurrection in Wheaton, Illinois, and Church of the Ascension in Pittsburgh, Pennsylvania, the two parishes that have felt most like homes to me, astonishing me with the joy and challenge of being a part of the body of Christ.

Thanks to my early readers, Laura DeBuys, Madelyn Johnston, Sari Ganulin, Carla Kuhlman, Jessie Epstein, and Hannah Cruz, whose feedback gave me clarity and encouragement while shaping the manuscript.

Thanks to Richard and Alison Gibson for the years of support and trust, and the talks of dreams at the kitchen table that you made feel like reality.

Many thanks to all at Paraclete Press for holding the poetry prize and being willing to publish a very green poet, and to judges Jon Sweeney, Mark Burrows, and Luci Shaw for selecting my work! Such an honor to be published alongside such wonderful poets, what a great gift.

Thanks to my family for constant love, a childhood full of art-making, play, and the firm foundation of learning the Bible. To my sister for joining me in my love of poetry and art, the long talks about what we're thinking about, to my mom for loving writing and teaching me to love it too, and to my dad for the underpinning of prayer and theology and paying close attention to small things.

Thanks to Bobo, my sweet big dog, warm writing companion, teacher of patience and giving, forcing me to go on way more walks than before.

And thanks forever to Isaiah, my husband, for the dailiness and steadfastness we keep learning together, the space and support that is unending and makes my work feel not only possible but real.

# about paraclete press

### Who We Are

As the publishing arm of the Community of Jesus, Paraclete Press presents a full expression of Christian belief and practice—from Catholic to Evangelical, from Protestant to Orthodox, reflecting the ecumenical charism of the Community and its dedication to sacred music, the fine arts, and the written word. We publish books, recordings, sheet music, and video/DVDs that nourish the vibrant life of the church and its people.

### What We Are Doing

BOOKS | PARACLETE PRESS BOOKS show the richness and depth of what it means to be Christian. While Benedictine spirituality is at the heart of who we are and all that we do, our books reflect the Christian experience across many cultures, time periods, and houses of worship.

We have many series, including *Paraclete Essentials*; *Paraclete Fiction*; *Paraclete Poetry*; *Paraclete Giants*; and for children and adults, *All God's Creatures*, books about animals and faith; and *San Damiano Books*, focusing on Franciscan spirituality. Others include *Voices from the Monastery* (men and women monastics writing about living a spiritual life today), *Active Prayer*, and new for young readers: *The Pope's Cat*. We also specialize in gift books for children on the occasions of Baptism and First Communion, as well as other important times in a child's life, and books that bring creativity and liveliness to any adult spiritual life.

The MOUNT TABOR BOOKS series focuses on the arts and literature as well as liturgical worship and spirituality; it was created in conjunction with the Mount Tabor Ecumenical Centre for Art and Spirituality in Barga, Italy.

MUSIC | PARACLETE PRESS DISTRIBUTES RECORDINGS of the internationally acclaimed choir *Gloriæ Dei Cantores*, the *Gloriæ Dei Cantores Schola*, and the other instrumental artists of the *Arts Empowering Life Foundation*.

PARACLETE PRESS IS THE EXCLUSIVE NORTH AMERICAN DISTRIBUTOR for the Gregorian chant recordings from St. Peter's Abbey in Solesmes, France. Paraclete also carries all of the Solesmes chant publications for Mass and the Divine Office, as well as their academic research publications.

In addition, PARACLETE PRESS SHEET MUSIC publishes the work of today's finest composers of sacred choral music, annually reviewing over 1,000 works and releasing between 40 and 60 works for both choir and organ.

VIDEO | Our video/DVDs offer spiritual help, healing, and biblical guidance for a broad range of life issues including grief and loss, marriage, forgiveness, facing death, understanding suicide, bullying, addictions, Alzheimer's, and Christian formation.

Learn more about us at our website:
www.paracletepress.com
or phone us toll-free at 1.800.451.5006

SCAN
TO
READ

# You may also be interested in these from Paraclete Poetry

## The Generosity
Luci Shaw

ISBN 978-1-64060-514-5
Trade paperback • $20

## Litany of Flights
Laura Reece Hogan

ISBN 978-1-64060-610-4
Trade paperback • $20

## Exploring this Terrain
Margaret B. Ingraham

ISBN 978-1-64060-376-9
Trade paperback • $19

# You may also be interested in...

## Accidental Grace
*Poetry, Prayers, and Psalms*
Rami Shapiro

ISBN 978-1-61261-655-1
Trade paperback • $22

## 99 Psalms
Said
Translated by Mark S. Burrows

ISBN 978-1-61261-294-2
Trade paperback • $17.99

## Midrash
*Reading the Bible with Question Marks*
Sandy Eisenberg Sasso

ISBN 978-1-61261-416-8
Trade paperback • $18.99